Aug 21

MOVERS,
SHAKERS,
& HISTORY
MAKERS

MILLICENT SIMMONDS

ACTOR AND ACTIVIST

BY RACHEL SMOKA-RICHARDSON

CAPSTONE PRESS
a capstone imprint

Capstone Captivate is published by Capstone Press, an imprint of Capstone.
1710 Roe Crest Drive
North Mankato, Minnesota 56003
www.capstonepub.com

Library of Congress Cataloging-in-Publication Data
ISBN: 978-1-4966-9540-6 (library binding)
ISBN: 978-1-4966-9716-5 (paperback)
ISBN: 978-1-9771-5466-8 (eBook PDF)
Summary: Deaf actor Millicent Simmonds captivated audiences with her performances in *Wonderstruck* and *A Quiet Place*. She has appeared in music videos, TV episodes, and at awards shows that have brought awareness to how deaf people experience the world. Learn more about this talented young actor and how she intends to give deaf people the space to tell their own stories.

Image Credits
Alamy: AF archive, 23, Ben Molyneux, 17, BFA, 29, Entertainment Pictures, 30; Associated Press: Invision for Producers Guild of America/John Salangsang, 39, Invision/Willy Sanjuan, 35; Getty Images: © ABC/Disney Channel/Fred Hayes, 33 (bottom), Joel Addams, 12, Michael Loccisano, 42, Nikki Beach/David M. Benett, 21; Newscom: BSIP/Jacopin, 14 (bottom), MEGA/KCS Presse, 7, Reuters/Pool/Christophe Petit Tesson, 13, TNS/Joan Marcus, 41, ZUMA Press/Daniel DeSlover, 37, ZUMA Press/Paramount Pictures, 26, 27 (bottom); Shutterstock: 4LUCK, 9 (top right), Artco, 9 (top middle), Debby Wong, 24, Featureflash Photo Agency, 19, Kathy Hutchins, cover (front), 5, 11, 32, lotan, 14 (top), Maxim Antonov, 10, 16, 18, 27 (top), 33 (top), M-vector, 9 (top left), Nazarii M, 9 (bottom middle), Rank Sol Graphics, 9 (bottom left), veronchick_84, 9 (bottom right), weedezign, cover (background), 1; Wikimedia: AgnosticPreachersKid, 43

Editorial Credits
Designer: Bobbie Nuytten; Media Researcher: Svetlana Zhurkin; Production Specialist: Katy LaVigne

Consultant Credit
Nancy Starr

Editor's note: In this biography, we've followed the National Center on Disability and Journalism's *Disability Language Style Guide,* which recommends deferring to the subject's preference on the use of "deaf" vs. "Deaf."

All internet sites appearing in back matter were available and accurate when this book was sent to press.

TABLE OF CONTENTS

Words in **bold** are in the glossary.

CHAPTER ONE

EARLY LIFE

Millicent Simmonds seems like a typical American teenager. She likes to read, listen to music, and hang out with her family in Utah. She does yoga, kickboxes, and walks her dog. She makes green smoothies but also loves red velvet cake and carrot cake. Her favorite subjects in school are history and English. Travel is one of her passions. She hopes to visit Egypt and see the pyramids someday.

But beyond that, Millicent is anything but typical. She has already starred in three major movies. The Disney Channel wrote a guest role specifically for her. She helped create a music video. She counts celebrities such as actors Julianne Moore, John Krasinski, and Emily Blunt among her friends. Millicent has let nothing stop her from chasing her dreams and achieving success.

Millicent at the 2019 Producers Guild Awards in
Beverly Hills, California

Millicent is an accomplished, hardworking person. She also happens to be deaf. But that is just one part of her identity, and only one reason why her achievements are outstanding. As Millicent said, "I'm an actress. I'm also deaf. . . . There's a lot more to me than just being deaf."

Born in March 2003, Millicent is the third of five children of Emily and Dustin Simmonds. She is sandwiched between two older brothers and younger twin sisters. "A lot of people say the middle child is the most adventurous," said Millicent. "That's me!"

FACT

Deaf pet owners can teach commands to cats, dogs, and other pets by using signs instead of spoken words. Animals can also be deaf; both deaf and hearing owners can use signs to communicate with their deaf pets.

Millicent at the *A Quiet Place Part II* premiere with her parents and brothers

Millicent wasn't born deaf. At around one year old, an accidental medication **overdose** caused her to lose her hearing. This changed the entire Simmonds family.

Her mother, Emily, had some prior experience with people who are deaf. Her aunt grew up deaf, but her grandfather refused to learn American Sign Language (ASL), a visual language communicated with handshapes, facial expressions, and body movements. The language barrier caused issues between Emily's aunt and grandfather. Emily did not want that to happen between her daughter and herself.

FACT

Millicent considers her mother to be her best friend. She also counts *A Quiet Place* costar Noah Jupe among her close friends.

CAUSES OF DEAFNESS

OVEREXPOSURE TO NOISE

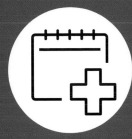

NATURAL AGING

FAMILY HEREDITY

HEAD INJURY

SOME MEDICATIONS

ILLNESS

Millicent's doctor told the Simmonds family that if they learned ASL, Millicent would get lazy and not practice her hearing. But it was important to Emily that the two of them have a strong relationship and be able to fully communicate. Emily learned ASL and then made sure the whole family could sign as well. As Millicent said, "It's harder for us to learn to speak than it is for hearing people to learn ASL. And we all don't lipread." Millicent communicates by ASL but does wear a **cochlear implant** to help her hear some sound.

ASL SIGN FOR "FAMILY"

Millicent wearing her cochlear implant at
an awards ceremony in Los Angeles in 2017

Bountiful, Utah, a suburb of Salt Lake City

The Simmonds family lives in Bountiful, Utah. Millicent is very close to her family. She rides motorcycles with her dad. She goes rock climbing with her brother and plays with and reads to her younger sisters. She is inspired by Malala Yousafzai, an activist for female education, and environmental activist Greta Thunberg. Millicent's family gives her courage, especially her mom, Emily. Millicent says that Emily is a strong woman who leads by example.

Emily encouraged Millicent to start reading at a young age. Millicent now loves to read, write, and tell stories. All of these are important skills for an actor.

Malala Yousafzai is a young Pakistani activist who advocates for girls' education rights.

HEARING AIDS

are battery-powered devices worn around or in the ears that make sounds louder. People can wear hearing aids in one or both ears.

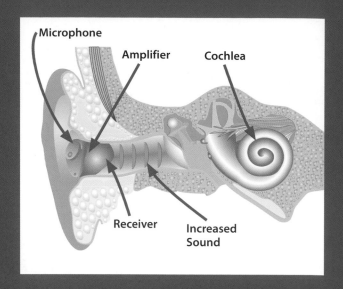

COCHLEAR IMPLANTS

consist of two parts: the receiver-stimulator (which is placed under the skin by surgery); and the speech processor, which is worn on the ear like a hearing aid. The two parts work together to capture sound and send it by electrical impulses to the **auditory** nerve. Millicent can listen to music with her cochlear implant.

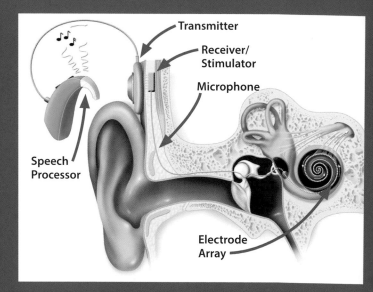

CHAPTER TWO

WONDERSTRUCK

Millicent didn't think she could become an actor because she never saw deaf people on TV or in the movies. Her plan was to someday become a firefighter or a police officer—a job with a little bit of danger involved. But she still liked to entertain people with her stories and **monologues.**

For elementary school, Millicent attended the Jean Massieu School of the Deaf. Her drama teacher noticed her talent for performing. Her first professional acting role was as Puck in William Shakespeare's *A Midsummer Night's Dream* at the Utah Shakespeare Festival. She then appeared with her mom in the student film *Color the World,* about deaf children and hearing parents.

ASL ALPHABET

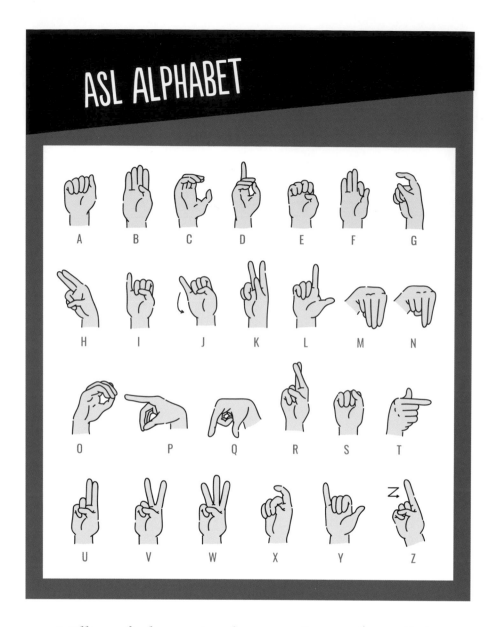

Millicent's drama teacher saw the casting call for a movie called *Wonderstruck*. It was based on a 2011 book for young people by Brian Selznick. One of its main characters, Rose, is a young deaf girl—around Millicent's age at the time. *Wonderstruck* was the first book Millicent had ever read that featured deaf characters. The drama teacher encouraged Millicent to audition for the role.

The production company sent Millicent some scenes from the movie. She practiced the scenes. Emily then used her phone to shoot a video of Millicent performing the scenes. Millicent was in competition with more than 200 other girls for the role.

Like Brian Selznick's earlier book, *The Invention of Hugo Cabret*, *Wonderstruck* is told in both words and pictures. Selznick was inspired to write the story after watching a PBS documentary about deafness called *Through Deaf Eyes*.

The production company was impressed with Millicent's audition. They flew her and her mom to New York to meet the movie's director, Todd Haynes. Millicent performed parts of the role in person for Haynes. Her performance was so moving that she made him cry.

The next day, Millicent and Emily were preparing to fly back to Utah. Before they left, Millicent found out that she had been chosen to play the part of Rose. Millicent and Emily screamed and cried with joy.

ASL SIGN FOR "PLEASE"

Award-winning filmmaker Todd Haynes directed *Wonderstruck*. He called Millicent "an exceptional person."

Emily, Millicent, and her sisters moved to New York during the filming of the movie. Millicent was nervous at first because she didn't want people to feel sorry for her. To her relief, the director treated her like everyone else.

Millicent grew close to actor Julianne Moore, who played her mother in the movie. "Millicent Simmonds is an extraordinary actress, I mean she really is," said Julianne. Millicent gave Julianne her own "name sign," something that only a deaf person can give to another person. Julianne's name sign is the signed letter J circling the face. The circle around the face means beautiful.

Julianne Moore and Millicent posed together in 2017. The first time Moore met Millicent on the set of *Wonderstruck*, she signed, "It's so nice to meet you, Millicent."

In *Wonderstruck,* the character Rose lives in Hoboken, New Jersey, in 1927. She is unhappy living with her mean, unloving father. She cuts her hair and runs away from home. Rose takes a ferry to New York City to find her mother, an actress.

Rose's scenes in the movie were filmed in black and white. They look and sound like the silent movies from the 1920s. The scenes have music but no talking. Millicent's favorite scene was cutting her own hair. She practiced on wigs over and over until she became comfortable cutting her own hair with her left hand using an old pair of scissors.

Wonderstruck's other main character, Ben, is also deaf. His storyline takes place in the 1970s. He runs away to New York City in search of his father. In the movie, Ben lost his hearing after being struck by lightning. He does not know ASL.

Millicent played the role of Rose in *Wonderstruck*. Her storyline was shot in black and white to mimic the era of silent films.

Hearing actor Oakes Fegley played Ben. To prepare for his role, Oakes put on headphones and walked around New York City with Millicent. Oakes got a small taste of how Millicent and other deaf people experience the noisy city of New York.

Young actor Oakes Fegley attending the *Wonderstruck* premiere in 2017

CHAPTER THREE

A QUIET PLACE

Shortly after the release of *Wonderstruck,* Millicent landed her second movie role. She was cast as the deaf daughter, Regan Abbott, in the horror thriller *A Quiet Place.* In the movie, the family fights cruel, frightening aliens. The aliens hunt their prey by sound, and the family survives because they know ASL. Their silent communication allows the Abbotts to hide.

The character of Regan is complex—she is brave and smart, but she is also stubborn and angry at times. She is determined to help save her family from the terrifying creatures that haunt their farmland.

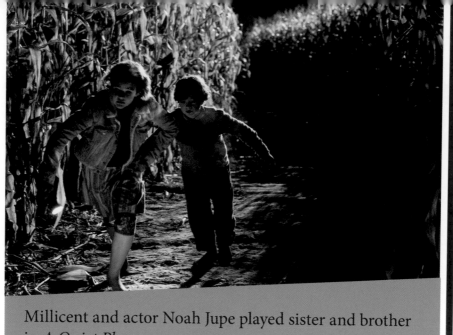

Millicent and actor Noah Jupe played sister and brother in *A Quiet Place*.

The screenwriters wrote the character of Regan as being deaf, and director John Krasinski insisted that they cast a deaf actress, specifically Millicent. Krasinski, who also played Regan's father, praised Millicent's acting abilities. "Special just doesn't cover it. Rarely in my career have I worked with someone more talented and professional than Millie."

A Quiet Place, released in 2018, was important to Millicent as it shows a hearing family that uses ASL to communicate with the deaf family member. She helped the cast learn some ASL for the movie. Krasinski regrets not learning more ASL as he thinks it's a beautiful language.

ASL SIGN FOR "YES"

Millicent as Regan, in a scene with director and actor
John Krasinski, who played her father

27

Also, Krasinski often asked Millicent about her experience as a deaf person so that the movie was **authentic.** Millicent hopes that the movie motivates other directors and screenwriters to include deaf actors and disabled actors in their work.

Millicent was nominated for the Critics' Choice Movie Award for Best Young Performer and several other acting awards.

Krasinski wrote the sequel, *A Quiet Place Part II,* with Regan as the lead character. Regan is able to help protect her family because of her deafness and ability to use ASL. Because ASL plays such an important part in the film, Millicent worked with an ASL coach to make sure that her signs were clear. Millicent used Regan's confidence as an inspiration to do her best.

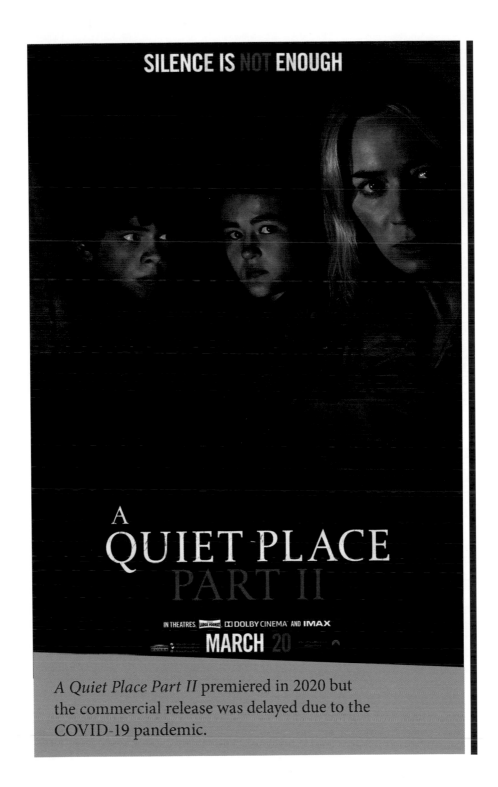

A *Quiet Place Part II* premiered in 2020 but the commercial release was delayed due to the COVID-19 pandemic.

Millicent in a scene with Noah Jupe and actor Emily Blunt in *A Quiet Place Part II*

Millicent loved being surrounded by beautiful nature at the filming locations in New York State. She said that the hardest part about filming the movie was the stunt work. Her favorite part about filming the sequel? Getting to work with her "movie family" again.

FACT

Millicent loves everything about acting, including traveling to new places, meeting new people, and the food on set.

CHAPTER FOUR

OTHER ACTING PROJECTS

Millicent's movie roles opened the door to other acting opportunities, including two guest-starring roles on television programs and a music video.

In its three-year run, the Disney Channel's show *Andi Mack* tackled a number of important issues. It was filmed in Salt Lake City, Utah. During its first season, it filmed an episode at Millicent's school, with Millicent and other students as **extras** in the background. The show's writers loved Millicent so much that they wrote a new character for her. Libby, the new girlfriend of series regular Jonah, appeared in two episodes of season three.

The cast of series regulars on *Andi Mack* at an event in Beverly Hills in 2017

The two episodes emphasized the importance of good, direct communication. Libby is upset because Jonah refuses to learn ASL, choosing instead to interact with her through texting or other students translating for him. Libby wants to break up with him. Then Jonah changes his mind and asks Libby to teach him how to sign.

Andi Mack also marked the first time Millicent had ever spoken on camera. When Jonah asks Libby to teach him ASL, she says, "I like you," then helps him sign it back. It shows a moment where the two characters appreciate and honor the other's usual form of communication.

ASL SIGN FOR "I LOVE YOU"

Millicent as Libby in an *Andi Mack* scene with the character Jonah, played by Asher Angel

Even though she was the newcomer, Millicent felt welcomed by the cast and crew of *Andi Mack*. She taught her costars some ASL, which was featured in the episodes. The producers chose to not subtitle the ASL shown in the episodes. They wanted the audience to pay more attention to the signing than the subtitles.

Millicent made another television appearance in the second season of *This Close*, a Sundance Now series. Deaf performers Shoshannah Stern and Josh Feldman created, wrote, and starred in the series. The main characters, Kate and Michael, are best friends living in Los Angeles and are both deaf. In one episode, Millicent plays Emmaline, a young deaf girl Kate meets while visiting her home in Georgia.

The team behind *This Close*, including deaf cocreators Shoshannah Stern (far left) and Josh Feldman (second from left)

Millicent got her break in music videos thanks to a fan of the electropop duo FRENSHIP. The fan asked that the music group provide an ASL interpreter at their live appearances. FRENSHIP asked Millicent to help create the music video for their song "Wanted A Name." They wanted to show how the song looks when communicated in ASL. In the video, Millicent walks through a beautiful landscape while looking at the camera and signing the lyrics. Their goal was to show audiences how some deaf people experience music.

FACT

Millicent's favorite musical artists include Father John Misty and the Red Hot Chili Peppers.

FRENSHIP performing at a Las Vegas music festival in 2017

CHAPTER FIVE

ALL ABILITIES IN THE MEDIA

Millicent has won a number of awards, including:

- Associated Press—one of Eight Breakthrough Entertainers, 2017

- Los Angeles Film Festival—New Wave Breakout Artist, 2018

- Greenwich International Film Festival— Make an Impact Award, 2019

- Hollywood Critics Association—2020 Next Generation of Hollywood Award

These awards are not only for Millicent's acting achievements, but her desire to change movies and television. She has taught directors and actors some ASL so they could communicate with her on set. And she has advocated for directors and screenwriters to include deaf people and people of all abilities in their work. In particular, she wants to see roles for people with disabilities "that you don't feel sorry for. We don't feel sorry for ourselves, so we don't need other people to feel that way about us."

Millicent signing onstage at the Producers Guild Awards ceremony in 2019

In 2019, the Greenwich International Film Festival hosted an event honoring Millicent for winning the festival's Make an Impact Award. A panel of experts discussed how important it is for deaf people like Millicent to play deaf roles in film and television. Actors of all abilities should be cast in roles authentic to their experiences.

The panel also said that television and movie creators should remember that audience members have a range of abilities as well. Millicent has watched the musical *Hamilton* multiple times. She praised its makers for doing a good job of providing captions to read on the screen. As Millicent has said, "We don't want to be left out. We want to laugh when everyone else is laughing. We want to be included."

In addition to writing and composing the musical *Hamilton*, Lin-Manuel Miranda was the first actor to play the title character.

Most importantly, Millicent wants to give deaf people the space to tell their own stories. She said, "I hope seeing people like me on screen inspires more people to chase their own dreams, and shows deaf kids anything is a possibility for them, because I really don't feel like my deafness was an obstacle or should be a big deal."

Millicent feels that it's important to advocate for deaf performers and creators during her publicity events.

HOW WAS ASL DEVELOPED?

1700s

Martha's Vineyard in New York had many deaf residents, and the townspeople created Martha's Vineyard's Sign Language, which both deaf and hearing people used to communicate.

1814

Minister Thomas Hopkins Gallaudet began to teach his neighbor Alice Cogswell, a nine-year-old deaf girl. He realized he needed to learn more about deaf education and traveled to Europe where deaf education was more advanced.

1817

Gallaudet cofounded what is now called the American School for the Deaf, the first public, free deaf school in the United States. At the school, what we now call American Sign Language was developed. ASL is rooted in both Martha's Vineyard's Sign Language and French Sign Language, as well as signs the students brought with them from all over the country.

TIMELINE

2003: Millicent Simmonds is born

2004: Millicent becomes deaf due to an accidental medication overdose

2006: Millicent begins attending the Jean Massieu School of the Deaf in Salt Lake City, Utah

2015: *Color the World* movie short is released

2017: *Wonderstruck* is released

2018: *A Quiet Place* is released

2018-2019: Millicent appears in two episodes of *Andi Mack*

2019: Millicent appears in an episode of *This Close*

Millicent stars in the music video for the song "Wanted A Name" by FRENSHIP

2020: *A Quiet Place Part II* premieres

GLOSSARY

amplifier (AMP-luh-fye-er)
the part of the hearing aid
that makes sound louder
and clearer

auditory (AH-dih-tor-ee)
related to the sense of
hearing or the body organs
used for hearing

authentic (ah-THEN-tik)
representing the truth about
a person or group of people

**cochlear implant
(CO-klee-er IM-plant)**
a device that is both
surgically attached to a
person's head and worn
around the ear; it helps some
deaf people hear

extra (EKS-truh)
an actor playing a small role,
such as a member of a crowd

**monologue
(MAH-nuh-log)**
a long speech performed
by a single person

overdose (OH-ver-dohs)
to take so much of a drug
that it causes harm

vibration (vye-BRAY-shun)
a motion or tremor caused
by sound waves

READ MORE

Adams, Tara. Illus. Natalia Sanabria. *We Can Sign!: An Essential Illustrated Guide to American Sign Language for Kids.* Emeryville, CA: Rockridge Press, 2020.

Bell, Cece. *El Deafo.* New York: Amulet Books, 2014.

Gino, Alex. *You Don't Know Everything, Jilly P!* New York: Scholastic, Inc., 2018.

Selznick, Brian, *Wonderstruck.* New York: Scholastic, Inc., 2011.

INTERNET SITES

ASL Kids: American Sign Language for Kids Resources
asl-kids.com

Deaf Unity: 8 Famous Deaf People Who Changed the World
deafunity.org/article-interview/8-famous-deaf-people-who-changed-the-world/

Sign Language For Kids
kidcourses.com/sign-language-asl/#

INDEX